2016 GREATEST CHRISTIAN HITS

ARRANGED BY
CAROL TORNQUIST

CONTENTS

Produced by
Alfred Music
P.O. Box 10003
Van Nuys, CA 91410-0003
alfred.com

Printed in USA.

No part of this book shall be reproduced, arranged, adapted, recorded, publicly performed, stored in a retrieval system,
or transmitted by any means without written permission from the publisher. In order to comply with copyright laws, please apply for
such written permission and/or license by contacting the publisher at alfred.com/permissions.

ISBN-10: 1-4706-3597-6
ISBN-13: 978-1-4706-3597-8

Cover photo:
Man in Field: © Shutterstock.com / Tom Tom

CALL IT GRACE

Words and Music by Chad Mattson,
Jonathan Lowry, Michael Farren and Seth Mosley
Arr. Carol Tornquist

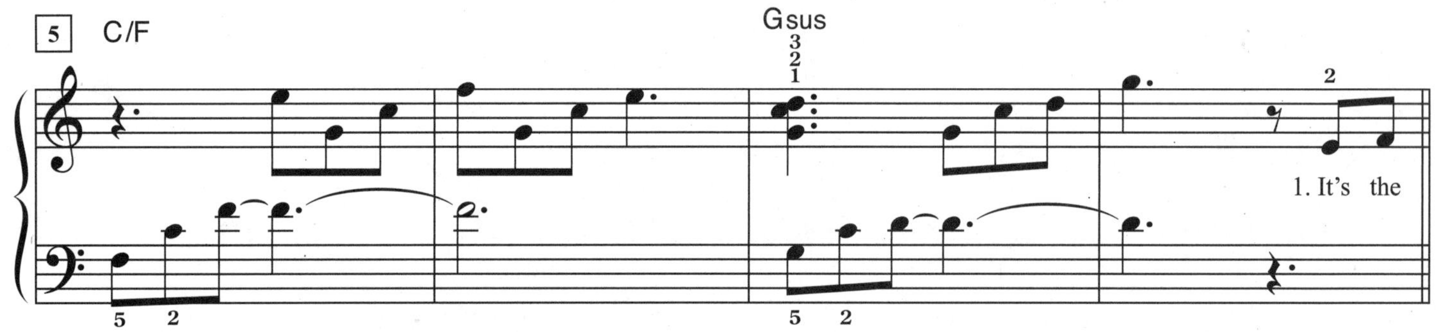

© 2014 FARREN LOVE AND WAR PUBLISHING, INTEGRITY'S ALLELUIA! MUSIC, CENTRICITY MUSIC and 2 HOUR SONGS
All Rights on behalf of FARREN LOVE AND WAR PUBLISHING and INTEGRITY'S ALLELUIA! MUSIC
Administered at at CapitolCMGPublishing.com
All Rights Reserved   Used by Permission

gen - tle hand that pulls you___ from the judg - ment of the crowd,___ when you
stand be - fore them guilt - y___ and you___ got no way out. Some may
Chorus:
call it fool - ish and im - pos - si - ble; but for
ev - 'ry heart it res - cues, it's a mir - a - cle.___ It's
noth - ing less than scan - dal - ous,___ this love that took our place. Just

Verse 2:
It's the breath that's breathing new life into what we thought was dead;
it's the favor that takes orphans, placing crowns upon their heads.
It's the hope for our tomorrows, the Rock on which we stand;
It's a strong and mighty fortress even hell can't stand against.
(To Chorus:)

EVER BE

Words and Music by Bobby Strand,
Chris Greely, Gabriel Wilson and Kalley Heiligenthal
Arr. Carol Tornquist

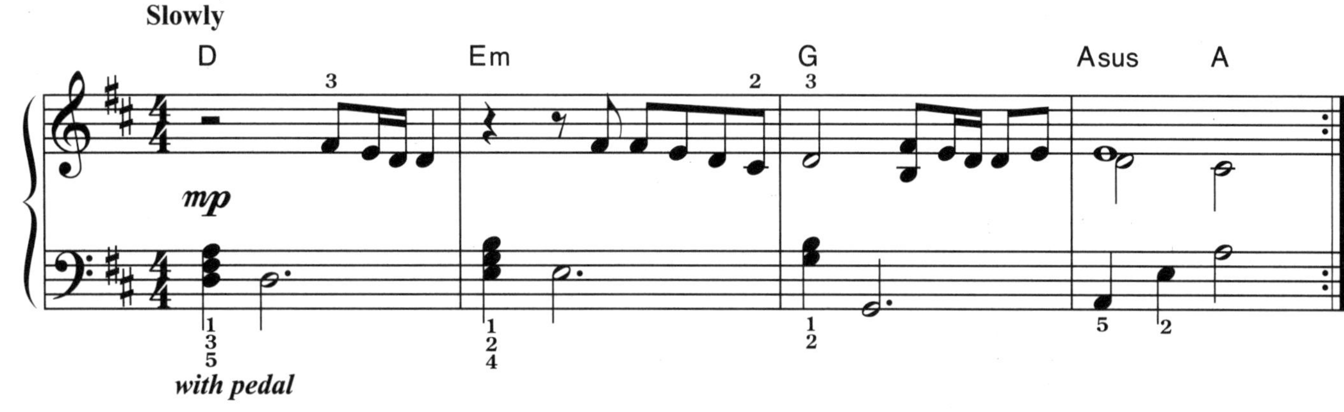

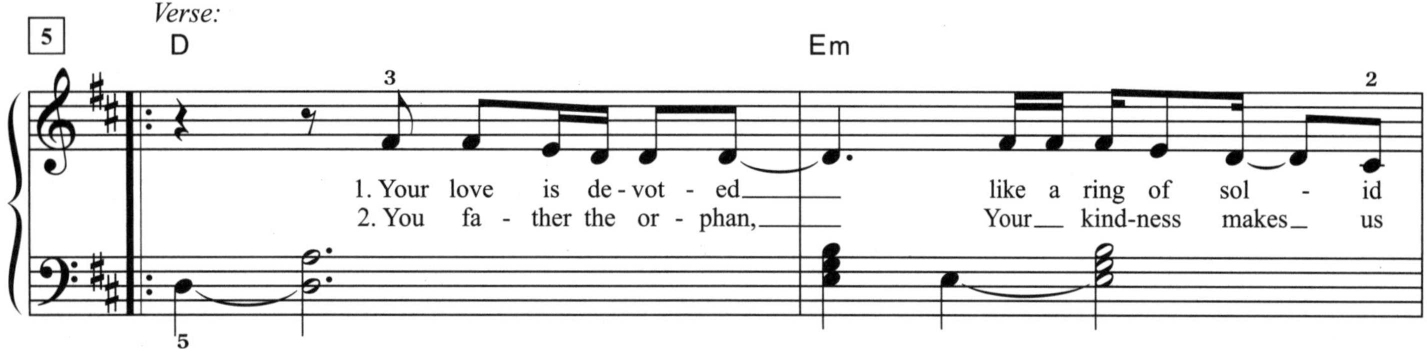

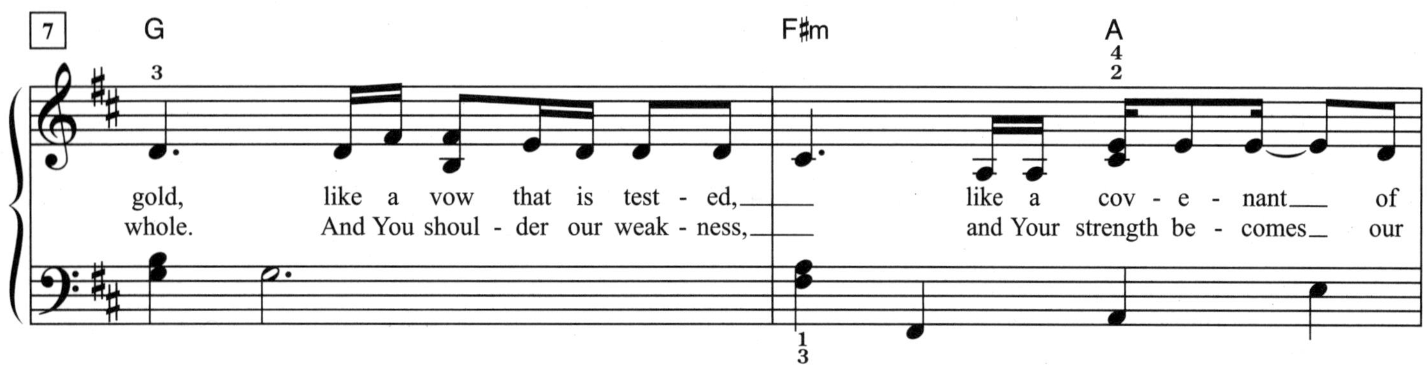

© 2014 BETHEL MUSIC PUBLISHING
All Rights Reserved   Used by Permission

11
G
F#m
A
rain
white,
and be-yond the ho - ri - zon
bring-ing beau - ty from ash - es,
with mer - cy for to -
for You will have Your

13
G
D
day.
bride,
Faith - ful You have been,
free of all her guilt
and faith - ful You will
and rid of all her

15
A
Em
be.
shame,
You pledge Your-self to me,
and known by her true name,
and it's why I sing:
and it's why I sing: Your

Chorus:
17
G
D
Bm7
praise will ev-er be on my lips, ev-er be on my lips. Your praise will ev-er be on my
mf

20
A
G
D
lips, ev-er be on my lips. Your praise will ev-er be on my lips, ev-er be on my lips. Your

23
Bm7   A   A7sus   D   A7sus
to Coda   1.
praise will_ ev-er be on_my lips, ev-er be on my lips.
2.
Bridge:
27
A   D   A
lips, ev-er be on my_lips.   You will be praised,   You will be praised._
30
Bm7   G   D
With an-gels and saints, we sing, "Wor - thy are_ You, Lord."_ You will be praised,
33
Em7   Bm7   G
You will be praised._   With an-gels and saints, we sing, "Wor - thy are_ You,
D.S. al Coda
36
D
Lord." And it's why I sing. Your
Coda
D   A7sus   D
lips.   rit.   mp

EVEN SO COME
(Come Lord Jesus)

Words and Music by
Chris Tomlin, Jason Ingram and Jess Cates
Arr. Carol Tornquist

© 2014 WORSHIP TOGETHER MUSIC, SIXSTEPS SONGS, S.D.G. PUBLISHING, SO ESSENTIAL TUNES and VISTAVILLE MUSIC
All Rights on behalf of WORSHIP TOGETHER MUSIC, SIXSTEPS SONGS and S.D.G. PUBLISHING Administered at CapitolCMGPublishing.com
All Rights Reserved   Used by Permission

15
D
1.
2., 3.
soon.
Chorus:
18
Em
C
G
Bm
f
Like a bride wait - ing for her groom, we'll be a Church read - y for
22
Em
C
G
Bm
You. Ev - 'ry heart long - ing for our King, we sing. E - ven so,
26
Cmaj7
Gsus
G
D
come, Lord Je - sus, come. E - ven so,
30
Cmaj7
Gsus
G
D
1.
D.S.
2.
come, Lord Je - sus, come. So we

10
Bridge:
35
C
Em
D
mp
wait, we wait for You. God, we
39
C
Em
D
wait; You're com - ing soon. So we
43
C
Em
D
wait, we wait for You. God, we
47
C
Em
D
wait, You're com - ing soon.
cresc.
Chorus:
51
Em
C
G
Bm
f
Like a bride wait - ing for her groom, we'll be a Church read - y for

Verse 3:
There will be justice, all will be new.
Your name forever, faithful and true.
Jesus is coming soon.
(To Chorus:)

GOOD GOOD FATHER

© 2014 COMMON HYMNAL DIGITAL, HOUSEFIRES SOUNDS, TONY BROWN PUBLISHING,
WORSHIPTOGETHER.COM SONGS, SIXSTEPS MUSIC, VAMOS PUBLISHING and CAPITOL CMG PARAGON
All Rights Administered at CapitolCMGPublishing.com
All Rights Reserved   Used by Permission

Chorus:
Fa - ther. It's who You are, it's who You are, it's who You are, and I'm loved by
You. It's who I am, it's who I am, it's who I am.
1.
Oh, and
2.
Be - cause You are
Bridge:
per - fect in all of Your
ways. You are per - fect in all of Your ways. You are per - fect in all of Your
ways to us. You are
3. Oh, it's

Verse:
love so un - de - ni - a - ble, I, I can hard - ly___ speak.
Peace so un - ex - plain - a - ble, I, I can
hard - ly___ think as You call me deep - er___ still, as You
call me deep - er___ still, as You call me
deep - er___ still in - to love, love,___ love. You're a good, good___

Verse 2:
Oh, and I've seen many searching for answers far and wide.
But I know we're all searching for answers only You provide,
'Cause You know just what we need before we say a word.
(To Chorus:)

IF WE'RE HONEST

Words and Music by
Francesca Battistelli, Jeff Pardo and Molly Reed
Arr. Carol Tornquist

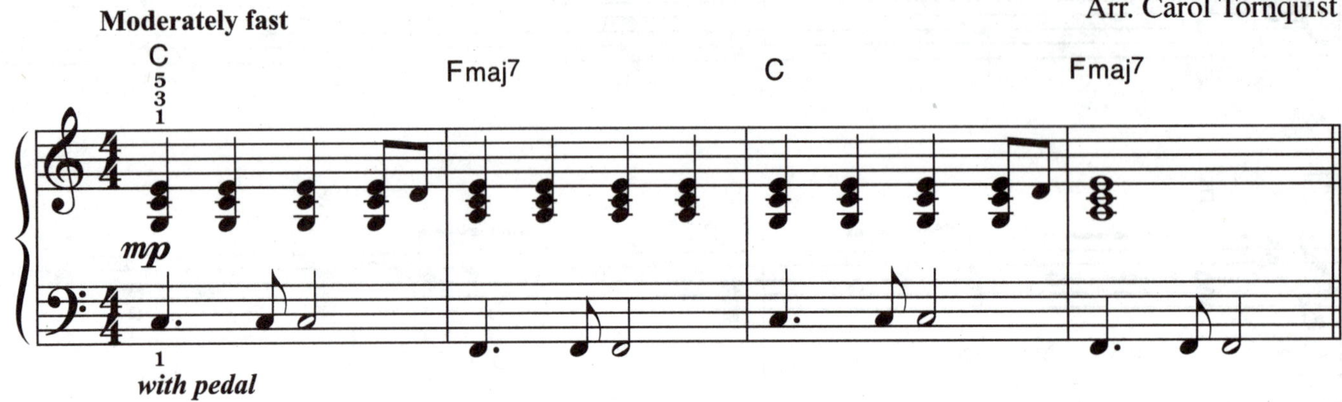

© 2014 MEAUX JEAUX MUSIC, DA BEARS DA BEARS DA BEARS MUSIC,
WARNER-TAMERLANE MUSIC PUBLISHING and WORD MUSIC
All Rights on behalf of MEAUX JEAUX MUSIC and DA BEARS DA BEARS DA BEARS MUSIC Administered at CapitolCMGPublishing.com
All Rights Reserved   Used by Permission

through. Yeah, it may be hard, but the best thing we could ev - er
do, ev - er do: Bring your bro - ken-ness, and I'll bring mine, 'cause
love can heal what hurt di - vides, and mer - cy's wait - ing on the oth - er
side, if we're hon - est. if we're
hon - est. 3. Don't pre - if we're hon - est,
Chorus:
mf
mp

18
35 F   C   F(add 9)
if we're hon-est.____
Bridge:
38 Am   E7/G#
It would change our lives,____ it would
41   G
set us free.____ It's what we need__ to be.__
44 D   C
47 Fmaj7   C   Fmaj7
So, bring your

Verse 3:
Don't pretend to be something that you're not, living life afraid of getting caught.
There is freedom found when we lay our secrets down at the cross, at the cross.
(To Chorus:)

JUST BE HELD

Words and Music by
Mark Hall, Bernie Herms and Matthew West
Arr. Carol Tornquist

© 2013 MY REFUGE MUSIC, ATLAS MUSIC PUBLISHING, BERNIE HERMS DESIGNEE and BE ESSENTIAL SONGS
All Rights on behalf of MY REFUGE MUSIC Administered at CapitolCMGPublishing.com
All Rights Reserved Used by Permission

Chorus:
13
C
G/B
on your knees and an-swers seem so far a-way,_ you're not a-lone._
15
Am7
Fsus2
C
_ Stop hold-ing on_ and just be held. Your world's not fall-ing a-part;_ it's fall-ing
18
G/B
Am7
in-to place._ I'm on the throne._ Stop hold-ing on_ and just_ be
20
Fsus2
Am7
Fsus2
C
Dm
held. Just be_ held,_ just be
23
Am7
Fsus2
C
G
C
G
to Coda
1.
2.
_ held._ 2. If your Lift your
rit. last time

Verse 2:
If your eyes are on the storm, you'll wonder if I love you still;
But if your eyes are on the cross, you'll know I always have and I always will.
And not a tear is wasted.
In time, you'll understand I'm painting beauty with the ashes.
Your life is in My hands.
(To Chorus:)

TELL YOUR HEART TO BEAT AGAIN

Words and Music by
Bernie Herms, Randy Phillips and Matthew West
Arr. Carol Tornquist

© 2014 AWAKENING MEDIA GROUP, ATLAS MUSIC GROUP and BERNIE HERMS
All Rights on behalf of AWAKENING MEDIA GROUP Administered CapitolCMGPublishing.com
All Rights Reserved   Used by Permission

Chorus:
Tell your heart to beat a-gain, close your eyes and breathe it in.
Let the shad-ows fall a-way, step in-to the light of grace.
Yes-ter-day's a clos-ing door, you don't live there an-y-more.
Say good-bye to where you've been, and tell your heart to beat a-gain.
been, and tell your heart to beat a-gain.
2. Be- been, and tell your heart to beat a-

Verse 2:
Beginning. Just let that word wash over you.
It's alright now, love's healing hands have pulled you through.
So get back up, take step one, leave the darkness, feel the sun,
'Cause your story's far from over, and your journey's just begun.
(To Chorus:)

OCEANS
(Where Feet May Fail)

Words and Music by Joel Houston,
Matt Crocker and Salomon Ligthelm
Arr. Carol Tornquist

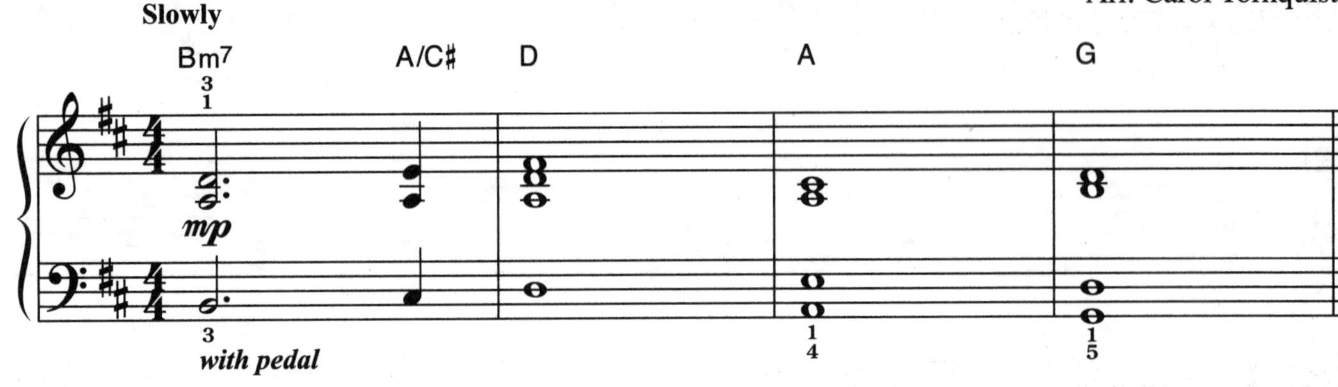

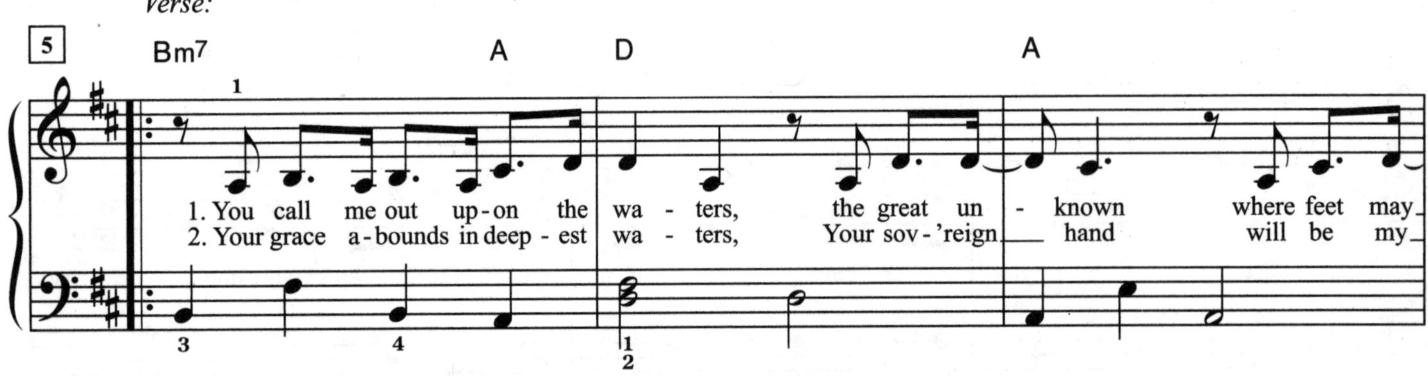

© 2013 HILLSONG MUSIC PUBLISHING
All Rights Administered at CapitolCMGPublishing.com
All Rights Reserved   Used by Permission

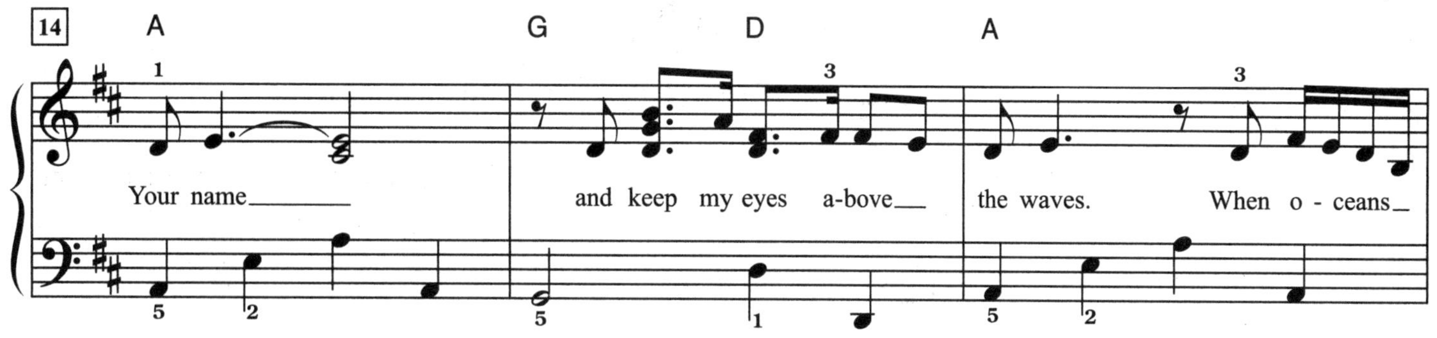
14
A
G
D
A
Your name____ and keep my eyes a-bove____ the waves. When o - ceans____

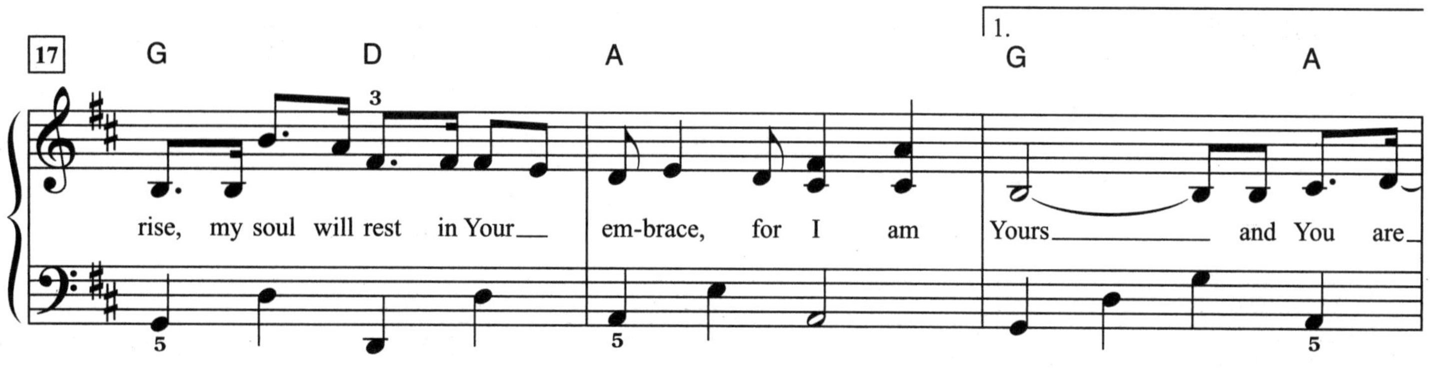
17
G
D
A
1.
G
A
rise, my soul will rest in Your____ em-brace, for I am Yours____ and You are____

20
Bm7
A/C#
D
A
G
____ mine.____

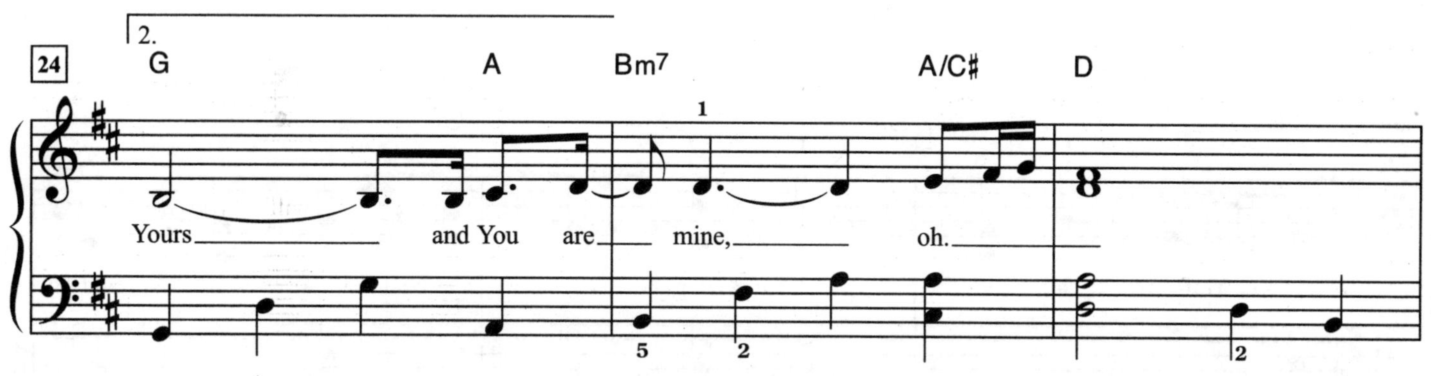
2.
24
G
A
Bm7
A/C#
D
Yours____ and You are____ mine,____ oh.

27
A
G
Bm7
A/C#
And You are___ mine,___ oh.___

30
D
A
G

Bridge:

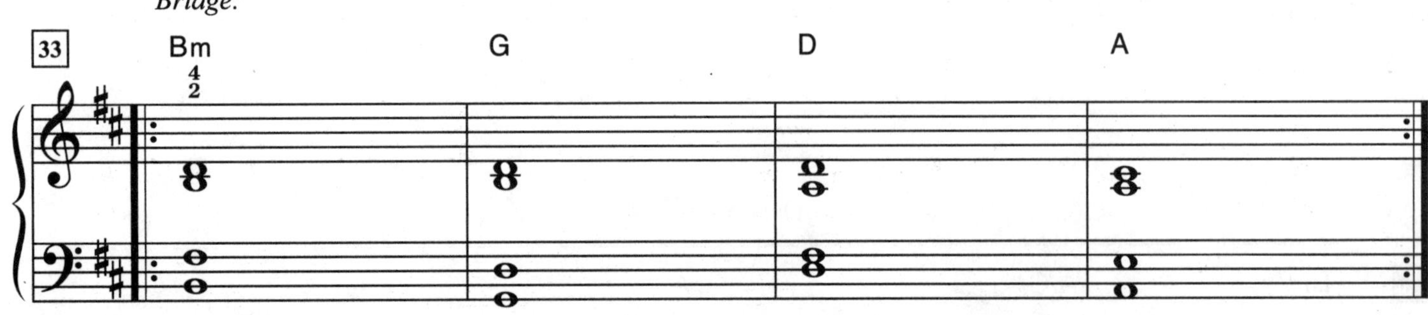
33
Bm
G
D
A

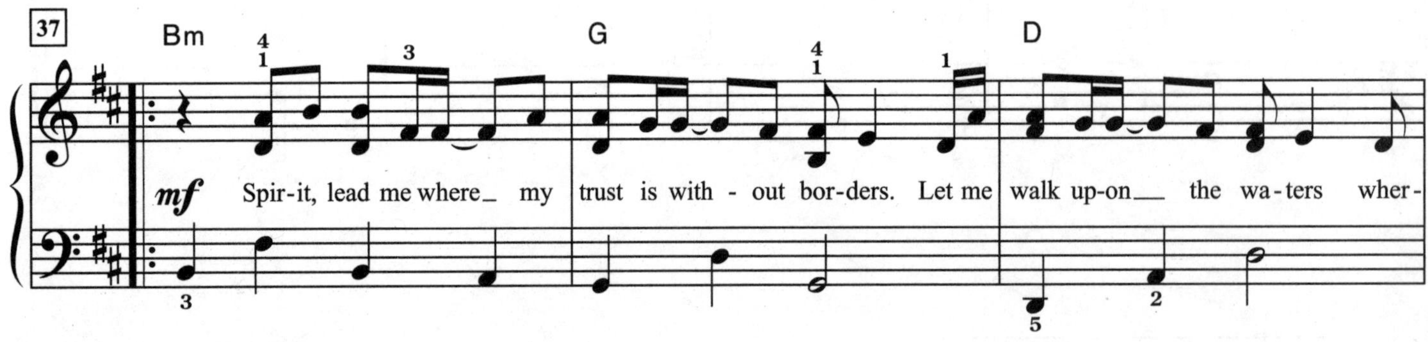
37
Bm
G
D
mf Spir-it, lead me where_ my trust is with - out bor-ders. Let me walk up-on_ the wa-ters wher-

40
A/C#
A7
Bm
G
ev - er You_ would call me. Take me deep-er than_ my feet could ev - er wan-der, and my

43
D
A/C#
A7
faith will be___ made strong - er in the pres - ence of___ my Sav - ior.
Chorus:
45
G
D
A
G
D
I will call up-on___ Your name________ and keep my eyes a-bove___
48
A
G
D
A
the waves. When o - ceans___ rise, my soul will rest in Your___ em-brace, for I am
51
G
A
Bm7
A/C#
D
A
Yours________ and You are___ mine.________
rit. e dim.
55
Em
Bm7
D
p

THE RIVER
(Come On Down)

Words and Music by
Jeff Pardo and Jordan Feliz
Arr. Carol Tornquist

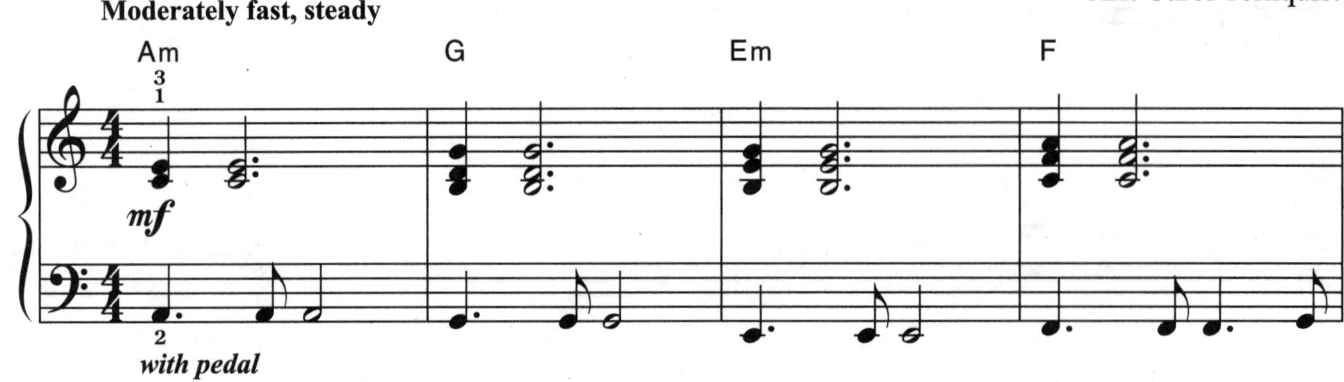

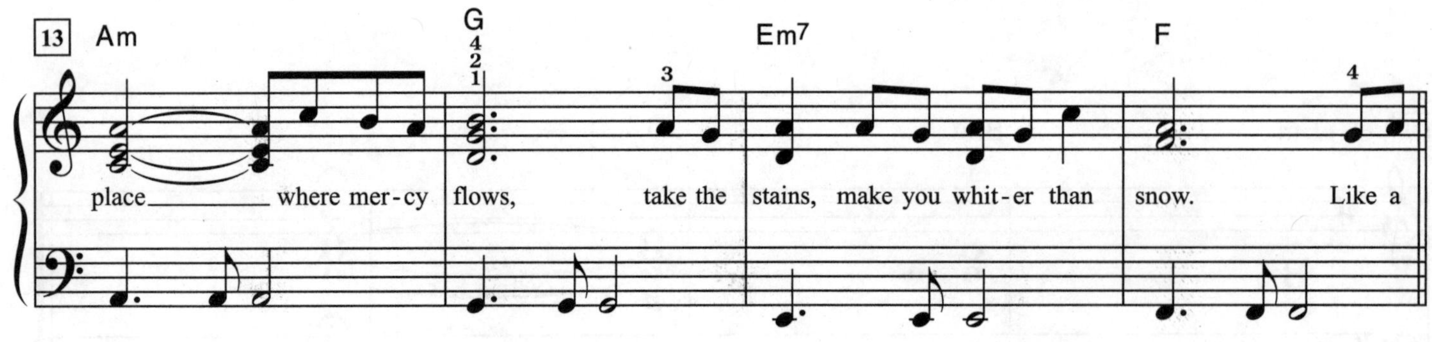

© 2015 MEAUX JEAUX MUSIC, DA BEARS DA BEARS DA BEARS MUSIC and ROYAL ENFIELD
All Rights on behalf of MEAUX JEAUX MUSIC, DA BEARS DA BEARS DA BEARS MUSIC Administered at CapitolCMGPublishing.com
All Rights Reserved   Used by Permission

Pre-Chorus:
Am
G
Am/C
tide,   it____ is   ris - in' up,   deep in - side,   a   cur - rent____ that   moves

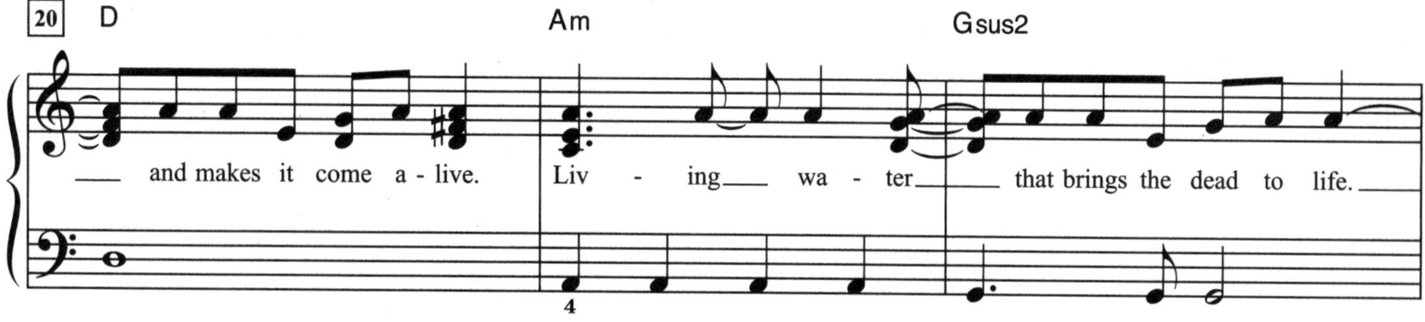
D
Am
Gsus2
____ and makes it come a - live.   Liv - ing____ wa - ter____   that brings the dead to life.____

Chorus:
C
D
Am
____ Oh,________   oh.   We're go - in' down   to   the riv - er,   down____

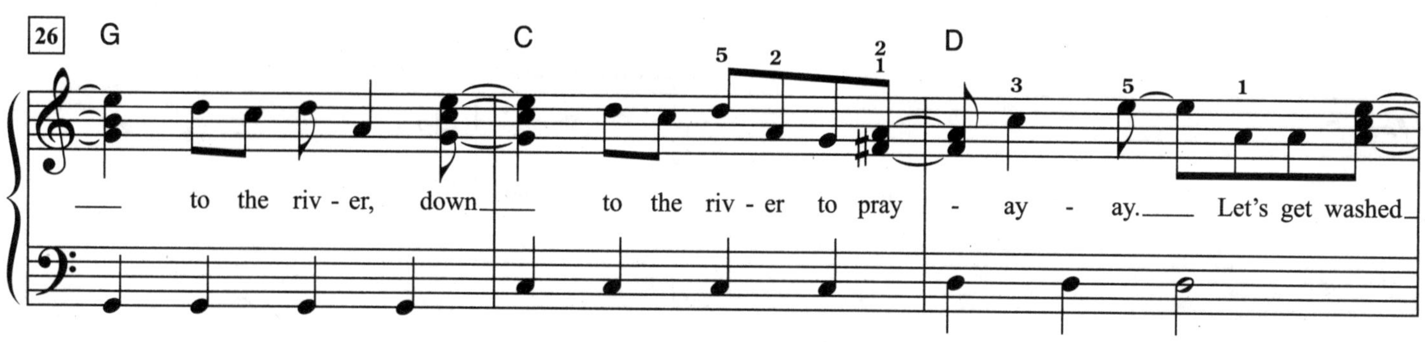
G
C
D
____ to   the riv - er, down____   to   the riv - er to pray - ay - ay.____ Let's get washed____

Am
G
C
____ by   the wa - ter, washed____   by   the wa - ter and rise____   up in a - maz - ing grace.

32 D   Am   G
Let's go down, down, down to the riv - er.

35 Am   D   Am
You will leave changed. Let's go down, down, down

38 G   Am   D   to Coda
to the riv - er. Nev - er the same.

Bridge:
41   Am   Gsus2
I've seen it move in my own life, took me from

44 Em7   F   Am
dust - y roads in - to par - a - dise. All of my dirt, all of my

47
G
Em7
F
D.S. al Coda
shame drowned in the streams that-'ve made me born a-gain. Like a
Coda
Am
G
C
Got-ta go, got-ta go,___ got-ta
53
D
Am
Gsus2
go down in a-maz-ing grace.
56
C
D
Am
Got-ta go, got-ta go,___ got-ta go down in a-maz-ing grace.
59
Gsus2
Am
molto rit.
mp

SLOW DOWN

Words and Music by
Chris Stevens and Nichole Nordeman
Arr. Carol Tornquist

© 2015 MOODY PRODUCER MUSIC, BIRDWING MUSIC, MEAUX MERCY and BIRDBOY SONGS
All Rights Administered at CapitolCMGPublishing.com
All Rights Reserved   Used by Permission

C
Am
G/B
ran, be-fore I knew it you were trying___ to free___ your fin - gers from my hand,
ran, be-fore I knew it you were teach - ing me___ the on - ly thing love can.
C
F
___ 'cause you could do it on your own___ now,
___ Hold hands through it; when it's sca - ry,
Chorus:
a tempo
Fm6
C
G
some - how.)
you've got me.)
poco rit.
Slow___ down, won't you stay___ here___ a min-ute more?
Am7
F
C
I know you want to walk through the door, but it's all too___ fast. Let's make it___
G
Am7
F
___ last___ a lit-tle while.___ I point-ed to the sky and now you want to fly.

I am your big-gest fan,
I hope you know I am,
but do you think you can some-
how slow down?
2. Here's to you.
Please don't roll your eyes at me. I know I'm em-bar-
rass-ing, but some-day you'll un-der-stand, you'll hold a

Chorus:
lit-tle hand,___ ask them if they can...___
Oh___________
'cause it's all too___
___ fast...
Oh___________
I am your big-gest fan.
I hope you know I am,
but do you think you can some-how___ slow down?

TRUST IN YOU

Words and Music by
Lauren Daigle, Michael Farren and Paul Mabury
Arr. Carol Tornquist

© 2014 FARREN LOVE AND WAR PUBLISHING, INTEGRITY'S ALLELUIA! MUSIC,
FLYCHILD PUBLISHING, SO ESSENTIAL TUNES and CENTRIC SONGS
All Rights on behalf of FARREN LOVE AND WAR PUBLISHING and INTEGRITY'S ALLELUIA! MUSIC
Administered at CapitolCMGPublishing.com
All Rights Reserved   Used by Permission

13
F#m7
Bm
my hands are wea - ry,_____ I need Your rest.
Might - y War - rior, King
16
D
of ___ the fight, _
no mat - ter what I face, You're by my side._____
Chorus:
19
A
E
F#m
When You don't_ move the moun - tains
I'm need - ing You to move,_
when You don't part the wa - ters_
mf
22
D
A
E
I wish I could - a walk_ through,
when you don't give the an - swers
as I cry out to You,_
to Coda
25
F#m
D
A
I will trust,_ I will trust, I will trust_ in You._

29
Verse:
3
F#m
3. Truth is You know what to - mor - row brings.
There's not a day a-head You have not seen, no.
33
Bm
D
5
D.S. al Coda
So in all things be my life and breath,
I want what You want, Lord, and noth - ing else.
Coda
A (add 9)
5
2
1
E
2
F#m
D
I will trust in You.
1
41
Bridge:
5
E
5
F#m
5
You are my strength and com - fort,
You are my stead - y hand,
You are my firm foun - da - tion,
44
D
4
5
E
the rock on which I stand.
Your ways are al - ways high - er,
Your plans are al - ways good.

47
F#m   E/G#   Chorus: A
There's not a place where_ I'll go   You've not al-read-y stood.   When You don't move the moun-tains
50
E   F#m   D
I'm need-ing You to move,_   when You don't part the wa-ters_   I wish I could-a walk_ through,
53
A   E   F#m
when You don't give the an-swers   as I cry out to You,_   I will trust,_ I will
56
D   A   E
trust, I will trust_ in You._   I will trust in You._
59
F#m   D   A
I will trust in You.   rit.   mp

THY WILL

Words and Music by Hillary Scott,
Emily Weisband and Bernie Herms
Arr. Carol Tornquist

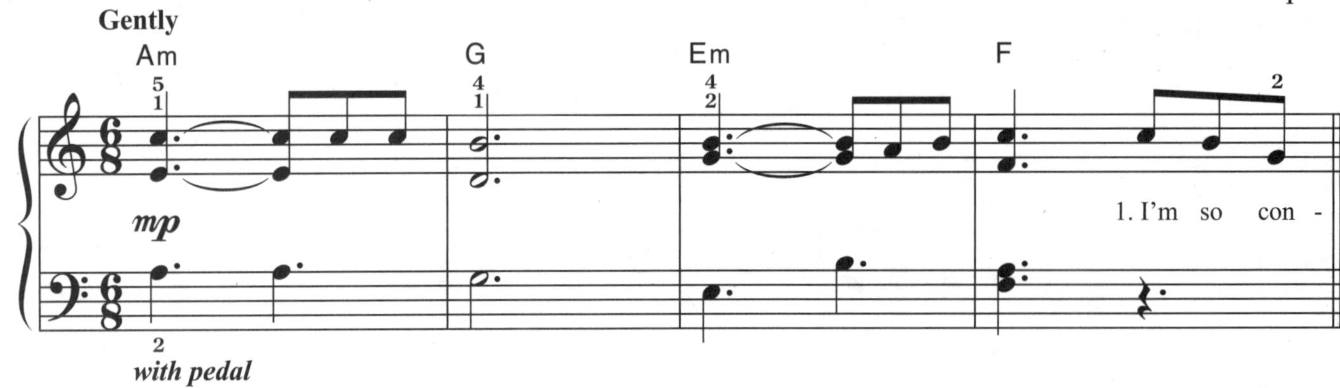

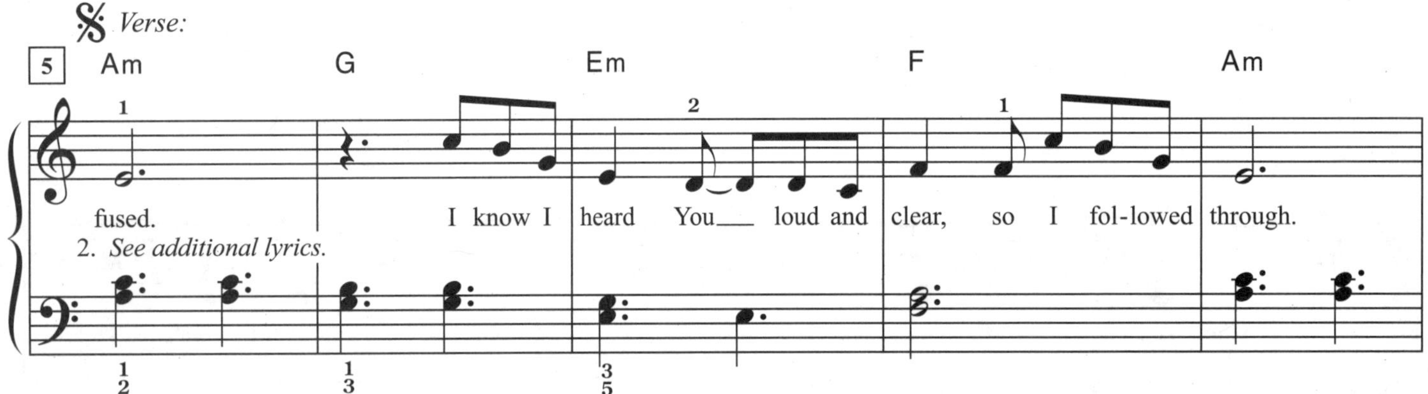

© 2016 EKT PUBLISHING, WB MUSIC CORP., THANKFUL FOR THIS MUSIC and SONGS OF UNIVERSAL, INC.
All Rights on behalf of EKT PUBLISHING Administered by W.B.M. MUSIC CORP.
All Rights on behalf of itself and THANKFUL FOR THIS MUSIC Administered by WB MUSIC CORP.
All Rights Reserved

17
Dm
G
When I try to pray,
all I got is hurt and these four words:
mf
Chorus:
21
F
G
Am7
Em7
F
to Coda
Thy will be done, Thy will be done, Thy
26
G
Am
G
Em
F
D.S. al Coda
will be done.
mp
2. I know You're
Coda
Gsus
Bridge:
F
G
Am7
will... I know You see me, I know You hear me,
35
Em
F
G
Am7
Lord. Your plans are for me. Good-ness You have in

Verse 2:
I know You're good, but this don't feel good right now.
And I know You think of things I could never think about.
It's hard to count it all joy, distracted by the noise.
Just tryin' to make sense of all Your promises.
Sometimes I gotta stop, remember that You're God and I am not. So,
(To Chorus:)